THE BEST 50
HOMEMADE
LIQUEURS

Dona Z. Meilach

BRISTOL PUBLISHING ENTERPRISES
San Leandro, California

Printed in the United States of America.

ISBN 1-55867-141-2

Cover design: Paredes Design Associates
Cover photography: John A. Benson
Food stylist: Suzanne Carreiro

MAKING HOMEMADE LIQUEURS

Making liqueurs and using them in marvelous ways can be done in your home, if you like to experiment, have fun and tackle new challenges.

People have made liqueur for centuries. As with many other homemade delicacies, industry stepped in and liqueur making became a highly mechanized process. Commercialism promoted the luscious liquids and surrounded them with an aura that they could only be made by highly technical procedures using impossible-to-duplicate secret recipes.

All this is so, with reservations. It is true that industrialized processes cannot be duplicated in the home. Exotic blends using scores of hard-to-find herbs cannot be copied perfectly by the do-it-yourselfer. But excellent simulations of popular and unusual liqueurs can be made — easily, cheaply and legally.

DEFINITIONS

Liqueur is derived from the Latin word *liquefacere*, which means "to dissolve." A liqueur is made by dissolving a flavoring agent in alcohol which is then sweetened.

Cordial is used interchangeably with *liqueur* in popular parlance. At one time it is believed the word cordial referred to fruit drinks flavored with brandy, but research on this is hazy.

Ratafia is also synonymous with liqueur and cordial. Its origin is believed to have been derived from the custom of drinking a toast when a treaty was ratified.

Eau de vie is a generic term for spirits made of fruits and alcohol that have been distilled with no sweetener added.

Fruit brandy is a distilled dry spirit made from the fermented mash of fruits. To avoid confusion, note that most liqueurs are flavored with the fruit essence; all fruit brandies *are* the fruit essence.

PRODUCTION PROCESSES

It is essential to understand the basic processes involved in making liqueurs: *distillating* and *macerating*. Distillating is the process of manufacturing alcoholic beverages using fermenting and distillation procedures. Whiskey is distilled from fermented "mash" made of corn, rye, wheat, malt, and other small grains and water. Brandy is made from the fermented juice of grapes and other fruits. Rum is made from fermented molasses and sugar cane juice. Distillation employs heat that extracts gas or vapor from the liquid to remove any impurities. When the necessary impurities are removed, and the liquid is rectified, pure alcohol results.

Macerating, the process most often used to make liqueurs, is essentially the same as *steeping*, the word used throughout this book. A flavoring substance such as soft fruits, herbs, spices, nuts or beans is placed in alcohol, usually vodka, brandy or whiskey. The flavoring is absorbed by the alcohol over a short steeping period of about 1 to 3 weeks and then the flavoring substance is strained or filtered out. Sweetener is added to result in the finished liqueur, which is allowed to mature, perhaps for 2 weeks to several months, to enhance the bouquet and the flavor.

LIQUEUR BASICS

The ingredients and equipment you need to make liqueurs are easily available and very uncomplicated.

INGREDIENTS

Flavorings

Flavor liqueurs with fresh or dried fruits, fresh and dried herbs, spices, nuts, beans, whole fruits, peels, pulp, seeds, roots, flowers and leaves.

Or use baking extracts: chocolate, mint, almond, vanilla, peppermint, etc. Always buy pure extracts, not imitation flavorings.

Concentrates for flavoring liqueurs are sold in wine-making shops and specialty food shops. "Noirot" and "Royal Piper" are reliable and available brands. Syrups for flavoring coffee, such as the "Torani" brand, may be used.

Alcohol Base

Liqueurs derive their character from the flavorings used, not from the alcohol base. Therefore, a flavorless base is usually most desirable, and vodka fills that requirement. Use the least expensive charcoal-filtered (it removes impurities) vodka available, and buy it in economy-sized bottles.

Most vodka in the U.S. today is 80 proof and ideal for making liqueurs. Proof refers to a mixture of alcohol and water containing a standard of alcohol of a specific gravity (0.7939) at 60°. In U.S. measure, this means the alcohol is double the percent in volume of the water. A 200 proof is pure alcohol; 100 proof means the mixture is 50/50 alcohol and water. Thus an 80-proof beverage would contain 40 percent alcohol and 60 percent water.

The addition of sugar syrup increases the ratio of water, thereby cutting the proof of the vodka. One cup of sugar syrup added to 3 cups of 80-proof vodka dilutes the alcohol to yield a 60-proof liqueur. When 2 cups of sugar syrup are added to 3 cups of 80-proof vodka, a 48-proof liqueur results (approximately).

Grain neutral spirits may be available in larger liquor stores in some areas. It is 190 proof and should be diluted half and half with water.

Brandy (80 proof) will blend well with a variety of fruit and herb flavors. Cherry brandy and apricot brandy recipes given are made by steeping the fruit in unflavored brandy instead of vodka; often a combination of vodka and brandy will result in an entirely different taste for the finished product.

Rum can be used for citrus flavors and for many berries. Whiskey and gin usually have their own individual flavors so must be used with discretion. They are the basis of Irish Mist, Drambuie and Cutty Sark. Experiment with them in small quantities to create your own mixtures.

Sweetening

Commercial liqueurs are almost always quite sweet, sometimes too sweet. Reducing the sweetness to your taste is one of the bonuses of making your own liqueur. A very sweet liqueur is usually termed a *crème*, such as crème de cassis or crème de menthe. A crème must contain at least 400 grams of sugar per liter (40%) in commercial production. A minimum sugar content of 200 grams is designated for French-made liqueurs (20%).

Use a ratio of 1 cup sugar syrup (8 oz.) to 3 cups (24 oz.) alcohol and adjust more or less to taste. (Sugar syrup is usually used for the addition as dry sugar does not dissolve easily in alcohol.) In most recipes, though not all, the sweetener is added after the flavoring and alcohol have steeped. To taste test, place 2 tbs. of the mixture in a small cup with 2 tbs. sugar syrup. Taste. If it is too strong, dilute by adding 1 tbs. of the liqueur at a time. If not sweet enough, add more sugar syrup. Aim for something like 2 parts liqueur to 1 part sweetener, 3 to 1, or 4 to 1, etc. Always record your additions carefully, and then transpose to the full recipe.

Always cool syrup before adding to alcohol mixture; heat causes alcohol to evaporate. If tap water is heavily chlorinated or bad tasting, heat the syrup for a few minutes to drive off chlorination. Distilled water may be used. For sweeter mixtures, use 2 cups sugar syrup. With experience, you'll learn to adjust the sugar ratio to your taste.

SUGAR SYRUP #1
1 cup white granulated sugar
1/2 cup water

SUGAR SYRUP #2
3/4 cup brown sugar
1/2 cup granulated white sugar
1/2 cup water

Bring to a boil, and stir until all the sugar is dissolved and the mixture is clear. Either recipe makes 1 cup.

A mild-flavored honey may also be used. Substitute 1 to 1 1/4 cup honey for 1 cup sugar syrup. Honey tends to cloud the liqueur, however. When honey is used, the mixture should be allowed to sit undisturbed for a few weeks; then the clear top solution is poured off or filtered.

Smoothers or Thickeners

Glycerin is used by commercial liqueur makers to give the product body. It is sold as a proprietary item on your druggist's shelf. Wine supply companies also market a prepared smoothing product composed of glycerol and sorbital. The addition of glycerin is optional; it does not affect the taste. It provides texture and adds a psychological effect.

Add about 1 tsp. glycerin or smoother per quart of finished liqueur.

Coloring

Many liqueurs are clear or light-colored amber and subtle earth shades depending upon the flavoring. To color liqueurs, add any pure food coloring sold for cooking and baking. The visual-taste sensation will have greater impact if a touch of yellow is added to banana, pink to cherry, green to mint. Use liquid or paste coloring very sparingly. Mix tiny droplets into a small amount of the liqueur, and then add the colored portion to the whole recipe until you achieve the shade desired.

A pinch of saffron in the steeping mix will turn it a beautiful yellow. For a green color, use a small amount of fresh spinach leaves, parsley or watercress. Place in a blender with a small amount of water and process finely. Add a drop or two of the resulting colored water to the alcohol mix. You don't want to add the vegetable flavor.

EQUIPMENT

Glass Bottles or Jars With Covers (do not use plastics)

- Use wide-mouth gallon and quart jars for mixing and steeping. Save empty jars from food products or use canning jars.

- Jars for aging can have narrow necks. For small recipes or dividing large recipes into two bottles, try dark bottles from beer. Always wash and sterilize used bottles in a dishwasher or by pouring boiling water into them to remove any residue from previous ingredients.

- Choose decorative bottles for serving or gift giving. Save decanters and bottles from commercial liqueurs, liquors and wines.

Measuring Tools

You will need measuring cups and measuring spoons, and a small kitchen diet scale that measures by ounce and gram.

Filter Materials

After the suggested steeping time, the solids used for flavoring must be separated from the liquid through a filtering process. Select filters of diminishing coarseness: wire strainers, cheesecloth, unbleached muslin, coffee filters, chemists' filters. The liquid is poured through 3 or 4 filtering materials beginning with a strainer or cheesecloth and graduating to muslin and finally a coarse or fine-grain paper filter. Use paper coffee filters or paper filters from chemists or pharmacies. Use a rubber band to secure filter cloth over a wide-mouth jar or support the cloth in a funnel and pour the liquid through. Pour any bottom residue into the filter cloth, grasp the cloth at the top, and twist it until all the liquid is squeezed through. When filtering, place the jar in a flat glass baking dish or pan; if you spill any of the liquid, you can retrieve it. As the filter material clogs, move it about or replace it as necessary. Discard or wash used filter cloths to avoid transfer of flavors from one liqueur to the next.

Sealing Materials

To seal the bottle well at every stage to prevent evaporation, use corks or screw-on metal lids with a layer of waxed paper under the cork or lid to help keep the jar airtight. Jars may be sealed with a layer of paraffin wax. Bottle seals may be used; they are tubes of a special material that are soaked in warm water and placed over the cork and bottle neck. When dry, the tube shrinks tightly around the bottle and cork and seals them.

PROCEDURES

There are two basic approaches for making liqueurs:

1. Steep (macerate) fruit, herbs, nuts, etc., in alcohol.

The mix is allowed to steep for several days, weeks or months. During this steeping period, the mixture is turned or shaken a few times a week. It is then strained and filtered. The sweetener is added to result in the clear, tasty finished liqueur. An aging or maturing period that helps to develop the full bouquet and flavor may require a few days or several months. Except when otherwise specified, the liqueurs presented in this book should be matured for several weeks or months. Taste is the real test.

2. Add flavored nonalcoholic concentrates to sugar syrup and alcohol.

All are prepared the same way, following specific label directions. Noirot and Royal Piper have been marketed for several years, as well as coffee syrups made by Torani and other companies. You'll find them in wine-making, gourmet and coffee shops. Use a 1-quart bottle and pour 2 cups sugar syrup (see page 7) into a clean, empty 1-quart bottle. Adjust the sweetness by reducing or increasing the amount of syrup. Add the concentrate and fill the bottle with vodka.

Steeping (macerating) fresh fruits in vodka requires only fruits, vodka and flavorings. Sweetener may be added after the steeping period. Concentrates are preflavored; they are poured into the vodka with the sweetener. They are ready to drink after about 24 hours — enough time to permit all the ingredients to blend.

To make 1 quart of liqueur, you will use less than 1 quart of vodka (about 3 cups), as sugar syrup and flavorings constitute some of the volume.

ELIMINATING CLOUDINESS

Cloudiness will not hurt a liqueur; it affects only its visual quality. Cloudy portions may be used for drinking or in cooking. To eliminate cloudiness, allow the sediment to settle at the bottom for a few days. Carefully pour the top clear liquid into another bottle so only the sediment remains in the original bottle. If this procedure is not successful, the clear liquid may be separated from the sediment by siphoning.

FRUIT FANTASY

To make a delicious fruit blend, add the fruits strained from mixes to a large glass jar or crockery pot. With each addition, place about 1/4 cup sugar into the jar along with about 1/8 cup vodka or brandy (or just enough to cover the fruits). Cover tightly. Store the jar in the refrigerator to prevent fermentation. Stir with every addition. Fresh fruits may be added. (DO NOT use herbs and spices with strong flavors which would overpower the fruits.) Serve *Fruit Fantasy* as a condiment with meat dishes or use it in cakes, puddings, pies, over ice cream and in parfaits. Keep adding to it and it will last indefinitely.

ABOUT LABELS AND RECORDS

Use a large label on the bottle to indicate the ingredients, amounts and date made. Also note the date to filter. Later, remove the label and transfer it to a notebook or file card with additional information including filtering dates, amount of sweetener added and your comments about taste.

COMMERCIAL LIQUEUR REFERENCE LIST

It is unlawful to make liqueurs and call them by their trade names. It is also impossible to duplicate specific brands, as they are made under highly guarded secret recipes and conditions. But it is entirely possible to simulate flavors in the liqueurs you make.

COMMERCIAL LIQUEUR	FLAVORING	CONCENTRATES AVAILABLE
Absinthe	Herbs, wormwood	
Advocaat	Egg yolks	
Amaretto	Apricot pits, almond	Amaretto
Angelica	Angelica, spices	
Anisette	Anise seed	Anisette (green/white)
Apricot	Apricot	Apricot
Aquavit	Caraway seeds	
Banana	Banana	
B & B (Benedictine and Brandy)	Herbs-angelica	Reverendine
Benedictine	Herbs-angelica	Reverendine
Bitters	Herbs, fruits	
Blackberry	Blackberry	Blackberry
Black Tea	Tea, spices	
Butterscotch	Butterscotch	
Calvados	Fermented apple juice	
Carlsberg	Herbs, mineral water	
Carmella	Caramel, vanilla	
Cassis	Black currant	Black currant
Cerasella	Cherry	
Chartreuse Green	Spices, herbs	Green Convent
Chartreuse Yellow	Spices, herbs	White Convent
Cherry Blossom	Cherry blossoms	
Cherry, Cherry Heering	Cherry	Cherry brandy
Cherry Marnier	Cherry	

COMMERCIAL LIQUEUR	FLAVORING	CONCENTRATES AVAILABLE
Cherry Suisse	Chocolate, cherry	
Chocolate	Chocolate, vanilla	
Cinnamon	Cinnamon	
Coconut, CocoRibe	Coconut	
Coffee	Coffee	Moka
Cointreau	Oranges, brandy	
Cranberry	Cranberry	
Crème d'Ananas	Pineapple brandy, vanilla	
Crème de Banana	Banana	Banana
Crème de Cacao	Cacao beans, vanilla	Cocoa
Crème de Café	Coffee	(see Kahlua)
Crème de Cassis	Black currants	Black currant
Crème de Cerise	Sweet cherries	
Crème de Cumin	Kümmel (caraway)	Kümmel
Crème de Fraises	Strawberry	
Crème de Framboise	Raspberry	Raspberry
Crème de Menthe	Peppermint	Green mint
Crème de Moka	Coffee beans, brandy	
Crème de Noix	Walnuts	
Crème de Noisette	Hazelnuts	
Crème de Noyau	Peach and apricot kernels	Sweet almond
Crème de Peche	Peach	Peach cream
Crème de Prunelle	Plums, prunes	Peach, prunella, pear
Crème de Poire	Pear	Pear

COMMERCIAL LIQUEUR	FLAVORING	CONCENTRATES AVAILABLE
Crème de Recco	Tea leaves, brandy	
Crème de Roses	Rose petals, vanilla	
Crème de Vanille	Vanilla	Vanilla
Crème de Violets or Yvette	Violet petals	
Cuervo Almondrado	Tequila (cactus sap), almonds	
Curaçao, Curaço Hollandais	Green orange peels	Orange red curaçao
Cutty Sark	Sweetened whiskey	
Danziger	Orange peels	Lorbuis, Danzig
Drambuie	Herbs, honey, whiskey	Lorbuis, Scotch heather
Forbidden Fruit	Grapefruit, brandy, oranges	
Frangelico	Hazelnut	Hazelnut
Galliano	Herbs, spices	Yellow Genepy, Italian Gold
Goldwasser	Lemon or orange peel, spices	Yellow Genepy
Grand Marnier	Orange	Orange brandy, Orange de Versailles
Irish Mist	Herbs, Irish whiskey, honey	
Kahlua	Coffee	Moka, Café Mexico
Kirsch or Kirschwasser	Fermented cherries	Kirsch
Kümmel	Caraway seeds	Kümmel
Malibu	Coconut rum	Coconut rum
Mandarine	Mandarin oranges or tangerines	
Maraschine	Maraschino cherries	Maraschino
Millefiori	Flower petals, plants	Floraues

COMMERCIAL LIQUEUR	FLAVORING	CONCENTRATES AVAILABLE
O Cha	Green tea	
Ouzo	Anise	
Parfait amour	Lemon peel, vanilla	
Peach	Peaches	
Peanut	Peanuts	
Peppermint	Peppermint	White mint
Pernod	Anise	
Peter Heering	Cherries	
Pineapple	Pineapple	
Piarxhi	Pistachio nuts	
Plum	Plums	
Prunelle	Plums, prunes	
Quince	Quince	
Rosemary	Herbs	
Sabra	Orange, chocolate	
Sambuco	Licorice, herbs	
Slivovitz	Plum	
Sloe gin	Sloe berries	Sloe Gin
Southern Comfort	Peaches, oranges, bourbon	
Strega	Herbs, spices	Stress
Tequila	Cactus juices	
Tia Maria	Coffee	Café Sport, Caribbean coffee
Triple Sec	Oranges	

COMMERCIAL LIQUEUR	FLAVORING	CONCENTRATES AVAILABLE
Van der Hum	Tangerine	
Vandermint	Chocolate, mint	
Wishniak	Cherry	Cherry brandy

MEASUREMENT CONVERSIONS

1 gallon	=	64 ounces	375 milliliters	=	12.7 ounces
1.75 liters	=	59.2 ounces	¼ liter	=	8.5 ounces
1.5 liters	=	50.7 ounces	1 cup	=	8 ounces
⅖ gallon	=	51.2 ounces	100 milliliters	=	3.4 ounces
1 liter	=	33.8 ounces	1 jigger	=	1½ ounces
1 quart	=	32 ounces	1 tablespoon	=	½ ounce or 3 teaspoons
750 milliliters	=	25.4 ounces			
⅘ quart (1 fifth)	=	25.6 ounces	1 dash	=	3 drops or 1/32 ounce
2 cups	=	1 pint or 16 ounces or ½ quart	1 millileter	=	⅕ teaspoon
⅘ pint	=	12.8 ounces			

CITRUS FRUIT LIQUEURS

Citrus fruits are almost always available. Try oranges, lemons, limes, grapefruit or combinations. They make popular liqueurs, and your guests will think you're an absolute genius when you serve your own variety of curaçao or Triple Sec.

There's really no way to make a mistake. If one liqueur is too sweet, add a bit of lemon to it and resteep. If it's too sour or bitter, add more sweetener. If the flavor is too weak, add more of the flavoring and repeat the steeping process or add ¼ tsp. of the necessary pure extract.

To enhance a basic flavor, add another flavor: a pinch of coriander, cinnamon, almond, caraway or lime peel, either to the original blend or after you have steeped and tasted the liqueur.

Take inspiration from commercial varieties and combine fruits with herbs, nuts and other flavors for such concoctions as orange with chocolate, coconut or cherry.

The inherent flavor of fruits can be unpredictable. They differ by type, where grown, the season and sweetness. Before sweetening, taste test (page 6) and add the sweetener tablespoon by tablespoon until a ratio is established. Remember, the greater the amount of sugar syrup added, the lower the alcohol content. This permits you to adjust the alcohol and flavor to create a tangy, piquant after-dinner drink, or a sweeter liqueur to mix into a variety of recipes.

Mix an *eau de vie*, made from flavoring and alcohol but not sweetened. It may serve as an addition to other liqueurs that need an extra touch of flavor. Simply set aside some of the flavored steeped mixes in bottles after filtering but without sweetening.

After sweetening, allow the liqueur to mature for at least a week before drinking; a month is better if your patience will permit. Storage periods tend to round out taste, flavor and brilliance and to allow the ingredients to interact, resulting in a bouquet and flavor characteristic of a good product. Liqueurs sweetened with honey will be cloudy. After maturing, the clear portion may siphoned off. The cloudy portion may be saved and used in cooking.

Orange peels are the basis for most commercially produced

orange liqueurs; the most popular are curaçao, Cointreau and Grand Marnier.

If you like to experiment, cut recipes in halves or thirds and steep some oranges in vodka, some in gin and some in brandy.

The flavor will vary depending upon the type of oranges used. The ripeness of the oranges and the season they are picked also result in variations of the final taste. Valencia oranges, for example, may be sweeter than California navel oranges. There are several varieties of Mandarin oranges — Dancy, Honey, Clementine, Kara — and all may be used. Always wash fruits thoroughly. Peels should be scraped so none of the bitter white membrane remains. Blot the peels on paper towels to dry off oils and water.

WHOLE ORANGE LIQUEUR

3 whole sweet oranges, cut into
  wedges
½ lemon

2 whole cloves
3 cups vodka
1 cup sugar syrup

Steep oranges, lemon and cloves in vodka (vodka should cover the fruit) for 10 days. Strain and filter. Add sugar syrup. Mature for 3 to 4 weeks.

ORANGE PEEL LIQUEUR

peels from 4 medium oranges,
  scraped, cut into large chunks

3 cups vodka
1 cup sugar syrup

Steep peels in vodka for 2 to 3 weeks. Strain and filter. Add sugar syrup. Mature.

Yield each recipe: 4 cups

Optional flavorings for orange liqueurs: 1 pinch or ¼ tsp. cinnamon; coriander; whole cloves; or a piece of lemon rind, scraped and cut

ORANGE JUICE LIQUEUR

1½ cups freshly squeezed
  orange juice
scraped, sliced peel of 1 orange

1½ cups vodka, or half vodka
  and half brandy
1 cup sugar syrup

Combine juice, orange peel and alcohol. Steep for 4 weeks. Strain and filter. Add sugar syrup.

ORANGE EXTRACT LIQUEUR

1½ tsp. pure orange extract
1 pinch cinnamon
1 pinch caraway

1 pinch coriander
3 cups brandy or vodka
1 cup sugar syrup

Mix all ingredients (including sugar syrup) and steep for a few days.

Yield each recipe: 4 cups

LEMON-LIME LIQUEUR

Liqueurs based on combinations of lemons and limes are particularly tasty in salad dressings as well as for sipping, and add zest and interest to other liqueurs. Experiment: Make a full recipe and sweeten half of the steeped fruit with enough sugar syrup to make it tasty. Use no sweetener or lightly sweeten the other half for an eau de vie. If you wish, substitute 2 tsp. each lemon and lime extract. No steeping or filtering will be necessary.

scraped, sliced peels of 4   3 cups vodka
  lemons and 4 limes   1 cup sugar syrup

Steep peels in vodka for 2 weeks. Filter. Divide into 2 separate bottles and add sweetener to 1 bottle only, if desired. Mature for 1 week.

Yield: 4 cups

DAIQUIRI LIQUEUR

This citrus recipe uses limes with rum as the base.

scraped, sliced peels from 4 limes
3 cups light rum
1½ cups superfine granulated sugar

Blot peel on a paper towel. Steep in 2 cups of the rum for 2 days or until rum absorbs color from peel. Remove peel. Add sugar and shake vigorously until dissolved. Add remaining 1 cup rum and stir until liquid is clear. Mature for at least 1 week.

Yield: 4 cups

WHOLE TANGERINE LIQUEUR

Tangerines make delicious liqueurs. A twist of lemon or lime peel helps to bring out the flavor. Make sure the fruit is covered with alcohol.

4-5 tangerines   3 cups vodka
4 cloves   1 cup sugar syrup

Pierce tangerine peelings. Insert cloves into 4 indentations. Steep in vodka for 10 days. Strain and filter. Add sugar syrup. Mature for 1 month.

Yield: 4 cups

TANGERINE BRANDY LIQUEUR

4 medium tangerines   3 cups brandy

Cut unpeeled tangerines into quarters and steep in brandy for 5 weeks. Strain and filter. Sweetener may not be needed with brandy. Mature quietly for 6 months before serving.

Yield: 3 cups

TANGERINE PEEL LIQUEUR

scraped, sliced peels from 5 medium tangerines
scraped, sliced peel from ½ lemon
3 cups vodka, or half vodka and half brandy
½-1 cup sugar syrup (depending on alcohol used)

Steep peels in alcohol for 3 weeks. Strain and filter. Add sugar syrup. Mature for 2 months.

TANGERINE VERMOUTH LIQUEUR

Add residue of steeped peels or fruit to 3 cups vermouth and let it stand for 6 months. (No sweetener is required.) Strain and filter. Mature for 60 days.

Yield each recipe: about 4 cups

Optional flavorings: 1 pinch or up to ¼ tsp. cloves; cinnamon; thyme; caraway seeds or coriander seeds

GRAPEFRUIT LIQUEUR

A well-known French liqueur called Forbidden Fruit is made from grapefruit and orange peels.

scraped, sliced peel from 2 grapefruits
3 cups brandy
½ cup sugar syrup

Steep peels in brandy for 10 days. Add sugar syrup gradually by tasting and establishing a ratio of flavor to sweetener. Grapefruit sizes and flavorings imparted by the peels and tartness vary markedly, so experimentation is required.

Yield: 3½ cups

PARFAIT AMOUR

This is basically a liqueur made from orange and lemon with fresh or dried flower petals (found in health food stores). The comparatively complex recipe can be easily simulated with pure extracts. This is traditionally a very sweet liqueur, but you can adjust the sweetness to taste.

1½ tsp. pure lemon extract
⅛ tsp. pure orange extract
½-inch length fresh vanilla bean,
 or ⅛ tsp. vanilla extract

6 fresh flower petals (carnations,
 hibiscus, lavender, orange,
 jasmine, rosehips)
3 cups vodka
1½ cups sugar syrup

Steep flavorings with vodka for 2 weeks. Remove vanilla bean and petals. Add sugar syrup. Mature for about 1 week.

Yield: 3-4 cups

FRUIT LIQUEURS

Using fresh fruits to make liqueurs is a challenging creative endeavor. The following recipes can be loosely interpreted and readily altered to please your own discriminating taste.

Most of the recipes that follow are made with fresh fruits. These cannot be exact, as variety, ripeness, natural sugar content and flavor of the fruits vary. Generally, the recipes should yield delicious results.

Frozen and canned fruits can be substituted for fresh fruits, but because of the variations in sugar and juices in different brands, it is impossible to develop a perfect recipe. You are urged to experiment.

Dried fruits, also excellent for liqueur making, should be plumped by placing them in boiling water to cover and allowing the fruit to sit in the hot water, with the heat turned off, for about 10 minutes until much of the water is absorbed. Pour off water. Cool completely and add to the alcohol.

Select fresh, ripe, firm fruit. In some recipes, the stones and pits are used. Dry sugar may be added to the fresh fruit and alcohol in the *initial* steeping; the sugar will chemically unite with the fruit to absorb it if the mix is placed in the sun or in a warm place and turned frequently. Or, the fruit can be steeped in the alcohol for a given period of time, and then strained and filtered and the sugar syrup added. Either process will be successful with most fruits and one can be relatively loose about the recommendations given. If you mix up the procedure, don't worry about it. Chances are the results will be delicious.

When steeping fruits, the alcohol should cover the fruit completely to preserve the fruit. If the amount of liquid given in the recipe is insufficient to cover the fruit, add a little more.

Dare to experiment with exotic fruits you may have available in your part of the country, or those growing on your bushes and trees. Even home-grown juniper berries can be delicious.

Whenever practical, save the strained fruits for *Fruit Fantasy*, page 12, or for use as they are in desserts and baked foods.

SWEET APPLE LIQUEUR

*Apples of many varieties are available year-round, so you can ex-
periment with recipes that range from the sweet, delicate flavors
of Red Delicious apples to the pungent, sharp flavors of Pippins.*

1 lb. Red Delicious or other sweet apples
2 cloves
1 pinch cinnamon
2 cups vodka or brandy
1 cup sugar syrup

Cut apples in halves or quarters and remove cores, but do not
peel. Steep apples, cloves, cinnamon and alcohol for 2 weeks. Strain
and filter. Add sugar syrup. Mature for 2 to 3 months.

Yield: about 3 cups

TART APPLE LIQUEUR

Use the strained liqueur-flavored apples from tart or sweet apple liqueurs for desserts. Combine them with freshly cut apples for pies and in sweet potato and squash recipes.

1 lb. slightly tart eating apples (about 3 average size)
2 cups sugar
2 cloves
1 pinch nutmeg
sliced, scraped peel of 1 lime or lemon
2 cups vodka or brandy

Cut ripe apples into about 8 pieces and remove cores, but do not peel. Place all ingredients in a tightly closed jar and set it in the sun for several days or until all sugar has dissolved and been absorbed. Strain and filter. Mature for 2 to 3 months.

Yield: about 3 cups

FRESH APRICOT LIQUEUR

A light almond flavor and aroma are subtly discernible, imparted from the nut inside the apricot pit or by adding crushed almonds or almond extract. Use vodka or 2 parts vodka and 1 part brandy.

1 lb. fresh apricots
3 cups vodka
1 cup sugar syrup

Cut apricots in half and remove pits. Place pits in a plastic or paper bag, and hit them with a hammer to open. Remove inner nut and discard shells. Place nuts in a bag and hit them to crush and release flavorful oils. (Any trace of the pit shell can impart a bitter taste.) Combine fruit and nuts in alcohol. Steep for 2 weeks, and shake gently 2 or 3 times a week. Strain and squeeze all juice from fruit. Filter until clear. Add sugar syrup. Mature for 2 to 3 months.

Yield: 3-4 cups

DRIED APRICOT LIQUEUR

*For créme d'apricot, double the sugar syrup in any apricot recipe. Add the strained fruit to your **Fruit Fantasy**, page 12.*

½ lb. dried pitted apricots
boiling water
5 whole almonds, or 1 tsp.
 almond extract

2-3 cups vodka or brandy
1 cup sugar syrup

Plump apricots (see page 29). Cool. Pour off any remaining liquid and measure; add enough vodka to make a total of 3 cups liquid. Combine liquid, apricots and almond. Steep for 2 weeks, shaking occasionally. Filter. Add sugar syrup. Mature for 1 to 2 weeks.

Yield: 3-4 cups

Optional flavorings: 1 pinch cinnamon or cinnamon stick; 1 pinch ground cloves or 2 whole cloves; 2- to 3-inch square fresh coconut, ¼ cup flaked coconut or 1 drop coconut extract; 1 small piece sliced, scraped lemon peel

BANANA LIQUEUR

Mix it dry or sweet, serve it in small glasses as a delightful aperitif, or pour it over ice cream; mix it with nondairy whip, or add it to the liquid when baking muffins, breads and cakes. For créme de banana, double the amount of sugar syrup in the recipe.

2 medium-size bananas, peeled
1 tsp. vanilla extract, or a 2-inch length vanilla bean
1 cup sugar syrup
3 cups vodka

Mash bananas and add vanilla, sugar syrup and vodka. Shake gently. Steep for 1 week. Strain and filter. It may be consumed now, but a 2- to 3-month maturing period will result in a richer flavor.

Yield: 4 cups

Optional flavorings: 1 pinch cloves; 1 piece cinnamon stick

BLACKBERRY, BLUEBERRY, ELDERBERRY, HUCKLEBERRY OR JUNIPER BERRY LIQUEUR

Use berries as freshly picked as possible. If frozen berries are substituted, compensate for the frozen juice by using less sugar syrup. You can mix fresh and frozen berries.

4 cups fresh berries
sliced, scraped peel of 1 lemon
1 pinch tarragon or cloves

3 cups vodka, or 2 cups vodka
 and 1 cup brandy or sweet
 white wine
1 cup sugar syrup

Lightly crush berries with a fork. Add to vodka with lemon peel and cloves. Steep for 3 months. Strain. Crush berries through filters to squeeze out all juices. Add sugar syrup to taste. Mature for 4 to 6 weeks.

Yield: 3-4 cups

FROZEN BERRY LIQUEURS

Many frozen fruits are sugared. For unsugared fruits, reduce the water in the sugar syrup because of the water content in the fruits.

1 pkg. (10 oz.) frozen berries   ¼ cup sugar syrup
1½ cups vodka, or part brandy

Add juice and berries to alcohol. Stir and steep for 1 week. Strain and filter. Taste. Add sugar syrup as necessary.

Yield: about 2 cups

CRANBERRY LIQUEUR

1 lb. fresh cranberries, coarsely   sliced, scraped peel of ½ lemon
   chopped   1½ cups sugar syrup
sliced, scraped peel of ¼ orange   1½ cups vodka

Add all ingredients to vodka. Steep for 4 weeks. Strain and filter. If needed, add more sugar syrup to taste and mature for another week.

Yield: 3-4 cups

RASPBERRY BRANDY LIQUEUR

For créme de framboise, use all brandy and 2 cups of sugar syrup.

1½ cups ripe raspberries
sliced, scraped peel of ½ lemon

3 cups brandy, or add part vodka
¾ cup sugar syrup

Lightly crush berries. Add lemon peel and berries to alcohol. Steep for 2 to 4 weeks. Strain and filter, squeezing all berries through fine cloth. Add sugar syrup and mature for 4 to 6 weeks.

RASPBERRY GIN LIQUEUR

This liqueur is ready to drink after you strain it.

2 lb. fresh raspberries, lightly
  crushed

2 cups sugar
3 cups gin

Mix all ingredients together. Turn every day until sugar is dissolved. Strain.

Yield each recipe: 4-5 cups

STRAWBERRY LIQUEUR

*Wild and cultivated strawberries will yield different flavors; wild
strawberries result in a stronger and more distinct strawberry
flavor if you are lucky enough to have them available. For créme
de fraises, add 2 cups sugar syrup.*

3 cups fresh strawberries, cut into thirds
3 tbs. confectioners' sugar
3 cups vodka
1 cup sugar syrup

Remove stems from berries. Sprinkle confectioners' sugar on
berries and let dissolve; add to vodka. Steep for 2 weeks. Crush
berries through a strainer. Filter. Add syrup and mature for 1 week.
Filter again through coarse to fine cloth and liqueur is ready to drink.

Yield: 5 cups

FRUIT LIQUEURS

CHERRY WISHNIAK

No sugar syrup is added, so the alcohol content will be high. The color is beautiful and the taste is divine. Whenever a recipe calls for whole cherries, pierce them to the stone. The alcohol should permeate to the stone, which imparts additional desirable flavor. Almost any fresh fruit may be substituted in this recipe.

½ lb. Bing cherries
½ lb. granulated sugar
2 cups vodka or brandy

Wash and stem cherries and place them on a towel to dry. Gently put cherries into a 1-quart jar. Pour sugar over cherries. *Do not stir or shake.* Pour vodka or brandy over sugar and cherries. Do not stir. Cover tightly with a lid and put the jar on a high shelf. Let it stand for 3 months without stirring or shaking. Strain into a 1-quart bottle. The cherry meat will be dissolved.

Yield: 2½-3 cups

CHERRY MINT LIQUEUR

You'll need a little sunshine to help this recipe along, but it's worth the effort, especially when cherries are in season.

2½ cups Bing cherries
10 cherry stones
10 fresh mint leaves, or 2 tbs. dried mint, or 1 tbs. mint extract
sliced peel of ½ lemon
2 cups vodka
½ cup sugar (not sugar syrup)

Remove stems from cherries, cut cherries in half and remove pits. Crush cherries lightly. Crush cherry stones by placing them in a plastic or cloth bag and hitting them with a hammer. Place crushed pits and cherries in a quart jar. Add sugar and vodka. Close jar tightly and place in the sun daily for 1 week. Set jar in a cool dark place for 4 weeks. Strain. Mature for at least 2 months.

Yield: 3-4 cups

Optional flavorings: 5 cloves; ½-inch stick cinnamon; 1 pinch mace

WHOLE CHERRY LIQUEUR

Save the strained cherries for desserts.

2½ cups Bing cherries
2 tbs. confectioners' sugar
sliced, scraped peel of ½ lemon

2 cups brandy
1 cup vodka
½ cup sugar syrup

Pull stems from half of the cherries. Cut stems from remaining half just at the top so the inner fruit is exposed. Pierce all cherries down to the stones with 4 or 5 holes. Place cherries in a quart jar. Sprinkle with sugar and let dissolve. Add lemon peel. Shake gently. Add brandy and vodka and cover fruit completely. Close jar and store in a warm place, about 75°, for 6 weeks, undisturbed. Strain and filter. Squeeze all juice from cherries. Add sugar syrup. Shake well. Mature for at least 1 week.

Yield: about 4 cups

Optional flavors: 5 cloves; ½ piece cinnamon stick; 1 pinch mace

CURRANT OR RAISIN LIQUEUR (CASSIS)

*Double the sugar syrup for créme de cassis. You can divide this recipe and make half cassis and half créme de cassis. Créme de cassis is commercially made with brandy, but it is also delicious made with vodka. Save strained fruits for **Fruit Fantasy**, page 12.*

1 cup water
1 cup dried currants or raisins

2 cups vodka or brandy
¾ cup sugar syrup for cassis

Boil 1 cup water. Add currants. Cover, turn off heat and let currants plump in hot water for about 5 minutes. Drain off water. Place currants and alcohol in a tightly closed jar and steep for 1 week. Shake jar occasionally during steeping. Strain and filter. Add enough sugar syrup for cassis, or more for créme de cassis, to your taste. Mature for 2 weeks.

Yield: 3-4½ cups

DATE OR FIG LIQUEUR

The fruits are inherently very sweet, so reduce the amount of sugar syrup and only add it in small portions as you taste it.

1 cup water
2½ cups (1 lb.) chopped pitted dates or figs, or combine 1 cup
each for a date-fig liqueur
2 cups vodka
¼-½ cup sugar syrup

Boil 1 cup water. Add dried fruits. Cover, turn off heat and let fruits plump in hot water for about 5 minutes. Drain off water. Cut fruit into smaller pieces with a scissors or a sharp knife. Place cooled fruit in vodka for 2 weeks; shake occasionally. Strain and filter. Add sugar syrup to taste.

Yield: 2½ cups

PAPAYA, MANGO OR MELON LIQUEUR

Papaya is a large, oblong yellow edible fruit grown in tropical climates. Its flavor is mildly sweet with a pleasant tang. Try mangoes and cantaloupes, crenshaw and honeydew melons, too.

½ medium-size ripe papaya, mango or melon
sliced, scraped peel of ¼ lemon or lime
1 cup vodka
⅓ cup sugar syrup

Cut fruit in half, remove peeling and seeds as you would a cantaloupe. Cut into ½-inch pieces. You should have about 1 cup. Place fruit pieces in vodka and steep for 1 week. Strain and squeeze softened fruit to extract as much juice as possible. Add sugar syrup. Mature for 3 weeks.

Yield: 1½ cups

PEACH LIQUEUR

Southern Comfort, an American liqueur, is based on peaches, bourbon and several secret ingredients. Add peach liqueur to mixed drinks, punches and a variety of recipes. The strained fruit is usually too soft to add to **Fruit Fantasy**, page 12. Keep it separately, add sugar, and spoon it over ice cream or eat it plain.

10 medium-sized ripe peaches   1 cup sugar syrup
3 cups vodka

Remove skin from peaches and discard skin and peach stones. Cut fruit into quarters. Place peach pieces in vodka in a tightly covered jar for 1 week and shake a few times. Filter and strain. Squeeze all juices from fruit. Add sugar syrup. Mature for 4 to 6 weeks.

Yield: 4 cups

Optional flavorings: 2-3 cloves; lemon peel

PEAR LIQUEUR

Any pear variety may be used for making fresh pear liqueurs (poire or créme de poire). If you like the liqueur sweeter, add sugar syrup in small quantities.

½ lb. mature ripe firm pears
peels only from 2 apples (any
  variety; Red Delicious is good)
1 clove
1 pinch cinnamon

1 pinch nutmeg
2 coriander seeds
1 cup granulated sugar
1½ cups vodka or brandy

Cut pears into strips (do not remove peel) and place in a jar with all dry ingredients including sugar and apple peels. Add alcohol to cover. Steep for 2 weeks. Shake jar every 2 days to mix ingredients. Strain and filter. Mature for about 2 months.

Yield: 1½-2 cups

PINEAPPLE RUM LIQUEUR

Fresh pineapples are tastiest when they are in season. They are delightfully sweet and juicy and easy to make into liqueurs.

1¼ cups ripe pineapple   3 cups rum

Peel pineapple and cut into small pieces. Place in a jar with rum. Steep for 3 weeks. Strain and filter. Mature for at least 1 month.

Yield: 3-3½ cups

PINEAPPLE BRANDY LIQUEUR

1 medium-sized pineapple,   sugar
  peeled, cored and thinly sliced   brandy

Place pineapple slices in a wide-mouth jar on top of one another. Add sugar until it reaches half the height of the fruit. Add brandy to cover fruit. There should be more brandy than sugar. Steep for 2 months. Strain and filter. Mature for 1 month.

PINEAPPLE VODKA LIQUEUR

2 cups fresh pineapple pieces
¼ tsp. pure vanilla flavoring, or
about 1 inch fresh vanilla bean, split
2½ cups vodka
½ cup sugar syrup

Combine pineapple, vanilla and vodka in a jar and let steep for about 1 week. Strain and squeeze out all juice from pineapple by mashing it through the strainer. Filter, sweeten with sugar syrup and filter through finer mesh filters, if any pulp remains. To make liqueur sweeter if necessary, add sweetened pineapple juice or small quantities of sugar syrup. Mature for 1 month.

Yield: 3-3½ cups

PLUM LIQUEUR

Enjoy the sweetened, liqueur-flavored fruit as a dessert.

1 lb. fresh plums, cut into pieces, with pits, or use whole plums
3 cloves
1 piece cinnamon stick, or 1 pinch cinnamon
1 cup sugar
2 cups vodka

Place plum pieces and pits or whole plums (pierce the skins to the pit) in a jar with flavorings, sugar and vodka. Be sure vodka covers plums. Steep for 3 months, shaking occasionally to mix ingredients. Strain.

Or, place plums and flavorings in vodka without sugar. Steep for 10 days. Strain and filter plums and add ¾ cup sugar syrup.

Yield: 3 cups

PRUNE BRANDY LIQUEUR

*Try this with flavored brandies such as grape, or a mixture of ⅔ brandy and ⅓ red wine. The strained fruits are excellent additions for **Fruit Fantasy**, page 12, but be sure to remove pits.*

½ lb. large prunes with or without pits
scraped, sliced peel from ¼ orange
1-inch piece cinnamon stick
¾ cup sugar syrup
2 cups brandy (or enough to cover prunes)

Place all ingredients in a jar. (It is not necessary to plump the prunes.) Steep for 4 weeks. Strain out prunes and set aside for a dessert. Filter liqueur. Mature for 2 to 3 months.

Yield: 2½-3 cups

HERB AND SPICE LIQUEURS

Experiments with medicinal plants by French alchemists during the Renaissance became the basis for many of the liqueurs we know today. Monks of the Carthusian, Benedictine and Cistercian orders appear to have dedicated their lives to the development of liqueur recipes that remain as guarded in this century as the day they were developed.

Many herb liqueurs are based on multiple flavorings with any-where from a dozen to a hundred ingredients. Best known are: *Benedictine* of France, which has a dominant angelica flavor; *Galliano* of Italy; *Grand Gruyère* of Switzerland; and the Spanish *Cuarenta y Tres (43)* which, logically, is composed of 43 herbs and plants.

Through the years, competitive liqueur producers have tried to imitate these well-known brands. Some have come close although, by law, none can use the same name. That is why you will find labels, such as *Dictine*, that are takeoffs from the trademarked brands.

Herb and spice liqueurs are easy to make with almost 100% success because the flavors remain the same and reliable.

The flavor potential of herbs and spices is quite strong, so minimal amounts are needed; as little as $1/4$ tsp. to 2 tbs., sometimes only a pinch of this and that. Taste preferences for these liqueurs are so varied that you may wish to make them in 2- to $2\frac{1}{2}$-cup quantities until you determine your favorites. Then double or triple the recipe.

Processed and dried herbs and spices should be as fresh as possible; long storage periods tend to dissipate the flavors. Watch them carefully as they sometimes attract tiny bugs.

Many herbs should be crushed or broken before they are used to release the flavors. Use a mortar and pestle or the back of a spoon against a cup. Or wrap the herb in heavy waxed paper and smash it with a hammer or rock. Some may be ground in a blender or chopped in a food processor.

If you have fresh herbs, substitute 1 tbs. fresh chopped herbs for $1/3$ tsp. powdered or $1/2$ tsp. crushed dried herbs.

PROCEDURE

Place the prepared herbs in the alcohol base for the specific length of time, usually a week or so. Shake the bottle and turn it over occasionally to keep the flavorings suspended in the alcohol. Strain out the herbs. Then add the sweetener. The addition of glycerin is optional.

All herb recipes should mature for a minimum of 1 month and up to 6 months, or as long as you can exercise restraint from tasting them.

One advantage of making herb liqueurs is that you can add more flavoring if a mix is too weak and let it resteep. If it is too strong, you can dilute the solution with more alcohol. Flavored extracts can be used in conjunction with the herbs.

ALLSPICE LIQUEUR

¾ tsp. allspice
1½ cups vodka or brandy

½ cup sugar syrup

Steep allspice in alcohol for 10 days. Strain and filter. Add sugar syrup. Mature for 1 to 6 months.

CINNAMON-CORIANDER LIQUEUR

2-inch piece cinnamon stick, or
 1½ tbs. ground cinnamon
1½ tsp. ground coriander seed
2 cloves

1½ cups vodka, or half and half
 vodka and brandy
½ cup sugar syrup (brown
 sugar syrup is good)

Steep spices in alcohol for 10 days. Strain and filter. Add sugar syrup. Mature for 1 to 6 months.

Yield each recipe: 2 cups

Optional flavorings: a few raisins or currants; 1 slice scraped lemon peel

ANGELICA LIQUEUR

Angelica is a species of the carrot family. Benedictine, Galliano, Strega and Drambuie all contain angelica.

½ oz. chopped angelica root or stems
½ oz. chopped almonds, or 1 tsp. almond extract
1½ cups alcohol
½ cup sugar syrup

Steep angelica and almonds in alcohol for 5 days. Filter and strain. Add sugar syrup or honey. Mature for 1 to 6 months.

Yield: 2 cups

Optional flavorings: 1 pinch nutmeg, mace or cinnamon; 1 clove; 1½ tsp. hyssop, lemon verbena; use any or all. Yellow food coloring optional.

STAR ANISE LIQUEUR

Make the liqueurs from anise seed, star anise and licorice root and let your own taste buds decide which you like best. Or make all three recipes and mix 2 ounces of each together in a separate bottle for heightened flavor and aroma. Very good.

2/3 tbs. crushed star anise
1 1/2 cups vodka
1/2 cup sugar syrup

Steep anise in vodka for about 2 weeks. Filter. Add sugar syrup. When completed place a whole star anise in a clear glass bottle as a visual effect and conversation piece; add liqueur. Mature for 1 to 6 months.

Yield: 2 cups

Optional flavorings: 1 pinch mace or cinnamon

HERB AND SPICE LIQUEURS

ANISE SEED LIQUEUR

$2/3$ tbs. anise seeds
$1/2$ tsp. fennel seeds
$1/2$ tsp. coriander seeds

$1 1/2$ cups vodka
$1/2$ cup sugar syrup

Grind seeds with a mortar and pestle and steep in vodka for 1 week. Shake frequently. Add sugar syrup. Mature for 1 to 6 months.

LICORICE ROOT LIQUEUR

$2 1/2$ tbs. chopped licorice root
$1 1/2$ cups vodka

$1/2$ cup sugar syrup, or to taste

Add chopped licorice root to vodka and steep for 1 week. Strain and filter. Add sugar syrup. Mature for 1 to 6 months.

Yield each recipe: 2 cups

GINGER LIQUEUR

Ginger-flavored liqueurs, like ginger snaps and ginger-flavored candies, are innocent enough on first taste; but after a few seconds, they pack a powerful aftertaste. It's a versatile herb that must be used cautiously and with a delicate hand. Other flavorings may be added.

½ tsp. dried ginger, or 1 tsp. grated ginger root
1½ cups vodka, brandy or whiskey
¾ cup sugar syrup

Steep ginger in alcohol for 1 week, shaking occasionally. Strain and filter. Add sugar syrup. Mature for 1 to 6 months.
Yield: 2¼ cups

Optional flavorings: 1 cardamom seed; 1 clove; 1 pinch cinnamon; a few raisins; ½ tsp. almond extract

KÜMMEL-CARAWAY LIQUEUR

*Kümmel, to those who know liqueurs, is almost synonymous
with caraway seed, from which it is distilled in commercial
production. But it can be made by the maceration process to
yield a dry, clear simulation of the real thing.*

1 tbs. caraway seeds	1½ cups vodka
1 whole clove	½ cup sugar syrup

Crush caraway seeds lightly with a mortar and pestle, on a board
or in a cup with the back of a spoon; add clove and combine with
vodka. Steep for 2 weeks. Strain and filter. Add sugar syrup. Mature
for 1 to 6 months.

Or to this recipe, add: 1½ tsp. fennel seed or anise seed, ¾ tsp.
ground cumin and 1 scant pinch black pepper.

Yield: 2 cups

MINT LIQUEURS

Double the amount of sugar syrup for créme de menthe.
Blot any oil from the surface with paper towels.

12-14 tbs. fresh, well crushed
   mint, peppermint or spear-
   mint leaves, or 6 tsp. dried
OR 2-3 tsp. pure mint extract

3 cups vodka
1 tsp. glycerin, optional
1 cup sugar syrup

With fresh or dried mint leaves, steep leaves in vodka for 10 days and shake the bottle occasionally. Strain and filter. Be sure to press all juices from leaves with a spoon against the strainer. Mature for 2 weeks. If using extract, combine all ingredients. Shake well. Mature for 24 hours minimum; 1 to 2 weeks will enhance the flavor.

If either recipe results in too weak a mint flavor, add more of the extract or leaves and repeat entire procedure.

Yield: 4 cups

ROSEMARY LIQUEUR

Keep the amount of rosemary scant, as it has a strong flavor.

1½ tsp. rosemary leaves, or 1 tsp. ground rosemary
1 mint leaf
scraped, sliced peel of ½ lemon
¼ tsp. coriander
1½ cups vodka
½ cup sugar syrup

Gently crush rosemary leaves and mint to release aroma and oils. Add lemon and herbs to vodka and steep for 10 days. Strain and filter. Add sugar syrup. Mature for 1 to 6 months.

Yield: 2 cups

SAGE LIQUEUR

In ancient times, the rather common garden plant sage was the symbol of wisdom; thus wise men are called "sages." In liqueur, it may be combined with other flavors for a distinctive drink. Divide the recipe in half if you prefer less yield.

12-14 fresh sage leaves, or 4 tsp. dried, or 2 tsp. ground sage
2 whole cloves
sliced, scraped peel of 1 lemon
1½ cups dry white wine
1¼ cups vodka
1 cup sugar syrup

Lightly crush sage leaves. Add cloves and lemon peel to white wine and vodka for 2 weeks. Strain and filter; add sugar syrup. Mature for 1 to 6 months.

Yield: 3¾ cups

PERSONAL POTPOURRI LIQUEUR

The history of liqueurs reveals that the early brews developed by the alchemists often contained an uncanny variety of rare and precious herbs and spices. Choose your own blend, using a pinch of each, such as cinnamon, nutmeg and sage; a few seeds such as coriander, fennel, anise and caraway; and 2 or 3 crumbled leaves such as mint, melissa, bay or rosemary. Add a clove. Result? Amazingly delicious.

3 tbs. herbs and spices
scraped, sliced peel of ¼ lemon
¼ tangerine or orange
a few dried currants

3 cups vodka, or half vodka and
  half brandy
1 cup sugar syrup

Steep ingredients in alcohol for about 2 weeks. Filter and strain. Add sugar syrup to taste. Mature for 1 to 6 months.

Yield: about 4 cups

BEAN, NUT AND EGG-FLAVORED LIQUEURS

Several aperitifs and after-dinner drinks that are usually considered liqueurs defy classification. They are made from a variety of beans such as cacao, vanilla and coffee, and nuts and eggs. Teas and flower petals are the basis for liqueurs as well, but there is not room to include them here.

Probably the most popular nut-flavored liqueur is almond, and *amaretto* liqueur is found under several labels. It is actually produced from the nuts found inside apricot pits, which have a strong bitter-almond flavor. You can make it with chopped almonds, extract or concentrates. The strained nuts are good in *Fruit Fantasy*, page 12.

Many of these delicious drinks can be simulated using the same maceration methods described earlier in this book. The alcoholic content can be raised or lowered by altering the amount of water added. Always buy the best and freshest quality flavorings you can.

COFFEE VODKA LIQUEUR

The Mexican Kahlua and Jamaican Tia Maria are probably the best known coffee liqueurs. Others are moka, mocha and créme de mocha. Coffee is among the easiest flavors to simulate.

2 cups water
2 cups white sugar
½ cup dry instant coffee

½ chopped vanilla bean
1½ cups vodka
caramel coloring, optional

Boil water and sugar until sugar is dissolved. Turn off heat. Slowly add coffee and continue stirring. Let cool. Add vanilla bean to vodka. Combine cooled sugar syrup and coffee solution with vodka. Cover tightly and shake vigorously each day for 3 weeks. Strain and filter.

Yield: about 4 cups

COFFEE RUM LIQUEUR

Substitute rum for the vodka for simulated *Tia Maria*.

Optional flavorings: 1 pinch cinnamon, cloves, orange peel, cardamom, mint

VANILLA BEAN LIQUEUR

Fresh vanilla beans are available in long glass tubes or folded over in jars. The fresh bean has a smooth dark covering and may be about 8 inches long with a soft lining that carries the flavor. When you open the tube, the scent is strong. A stale bean looks like a piece of dried beef and has shrunk to about half the size; the vanilla smell is stale. Pure vanilla extract may be substituted.

2 fresh whole vanilla beans, about 5 inches long
1½ cups vodka
½ cup sugar syrup

Steep vanilla beans in vodka and be sure they are immersed. Shake well and steep for 2 to 3 weeks. Remove beans and filter if necessary. Add sugar syrup. Mature for about 1 month.

Yield: 2 cups

VANILLA EXTRACT LIQUEUR

Vanilla is frequently used in conjunction with other flavorings and especially with cacao beans for the popular créme de cacao. Carmella is a liqueur with a combination of caramel and vanilla.

1½ tsp. pure vanilla extract (or dried or ground vanilla)
1 pinch cinnamon
1½ cups vodka or brandy
½ cup sugar syrup

Mix vanilla and alcohol and shake well. Steep for 1 week. Add sugar syrup to the solution; no straining will be required. If you use dried or ground vanilla, the solution should be filtered before adding sugar syrup. Mature for at least 1 week.

Yield: 2 cups

CHOCOLATE LIQUEUR

Chocolate liqueurs are usually a blend of the cocoa bean with a proportion of vanilla pods. The distillation of the cocoa bean is a clear liquid which is colored brown in the production process. Homemade chocolate liqueurs and blends do not seem as rich-bodied as those made commercially, such as Vandermint and cherry suisse, but they are an adequate substitute and much less costly. Mix finished liqueurs together for blends such as chocolate-orange, chocolate coconut and chocolate cherry and mature for 2 weeks for best flavors.

2 tsp. pure chocolate extract
  used for baking
½ tsp. pure vanilla extract

1½ cups vodka
½ cup sugar syrup

Mix all the ingredients together and mature for several days.

Yield: 2 cups

PEANUT LIQUEUR

All nut recipes are made the same way. Only the type of nut and the added flavorings create different tastes. Try your favorites steeped in vodka or brandy. Add a trace of other compatible flavorings, such as chocolate and raisins. For a downright decadent adventure, try this.

4 oz. fresh unsalted, unroasted
  peanuts, shelled
3-inch piece vanilla bean, or
  ¼ tsp. vanilla extract

1½ cups vodka
½ cup sugar syrup

Chop peanuts slightly and add with vanilla to vodka. Steep for 2 weeks. Strain and filter. Add sugar syrup and mature for 2 months.

Yield: 2 cups

WALNUT OR PISTACHIO LIQUEUR

If you are unsure about flavorings that go well with a certain nut, refer to cookbooks to find recipes for cookies or desserts and check the combinations. For example, a walnut dessert recipe might call for vanilla, or cinnamon, cloves and raisins.

3-4 oz. chopped black walnuts or pistachio nuts
1 pinch cinnamon
1 pinch cloves
12 raisins or currants, optional
1½ cups vodka
½ cup sugar syrup

Steep nuts, raisins and spices in vodka for 2 weeks. Shake occasionally. Strain and filter. Add sugar syrup. Mature for 2 to 3 weeks.

Yield: about 2-2½ cups

FRESH COCONUT LIQUEUR

*Coconut has an unusually large amount of natural sugar and this
liqueur may not require any sugar syrup. Try it mixed with
orange or vanilla, too.*

12 oz. fresh coconut, white meaty portion
3 coriander seeds
1-inch piece vanilla bean, or 1 drop vanilla extract
10 oz. vodka
3 oz. brandy

Cut coconut meat into small pieces or grate on a large grater and
combine with remaining ingredients. Steep for 3 weeks and shake it
gently every 3 to 4 days. Strain and filter. If sugar syrup is required,
add 1 to 2 oz. at a time rather than by ½ cups. Mature for 2 to 3 weeks.

Yield: about 2 cups

ALMOND EXTRACT LIQUEUR

½ tsp. pure almond extract   ½ cup sugar syrup
1½ cups vodka

Add all ingredients together and shake well. Mature for several days.

CHOPPED ALMOND LIQUEUR

Chop fresh unblanched, unsalted almonds coarsely to release flavorful oils. If too finely chopped, they are difficult to filter.

3 oz. chopped almonds   1½ cups vodka
1 pinch cinnamon   ½ cup sugar syrup

Combine all ingredients, shake well and steep for about 2 weeks. Filter. Sweeten. Mature for 2 to 3 weeks.

Yield each recipe: 2 cups

EGG LIQUEUR

Liqueurs made from eggs are a European delight, and excellent for baking and cooking. Advocaat is a thick sweet egg yolk and brandy emulsion. This is delicious by itself, in baking recipes and added to eggnog. After opening, the shelf life is about 5 months in a cool place.

8 egg yolks
2 drops vanilla extract
1 cup sugar
1 can (15 oz.) condensed milk
20 oz. brandy, or ⅔ brandy, ⅓ vodka

Beat egg yolks, vanilla and sugar until pale lemon colored at medium speed with a mixer or by hand. While beating, add milk slowly. Add alcohol and stir thoroughly. Put in a tightly covered bottle and store in a cool, dark place unopened for 1 year.

Yield: about 4½ cups

EGG LIQUEUR WITH MARSALA WINE

Another European recipe results in a rich, creamy liqueur that tastes like the filling of Italian pastries. It makes an excellent sauce for cream puffs, ice cream and cakes.

5 egg yolks
1½ cups sugar
1 cup milk

1 cup dry Marsala wine
½ tsp. vanilla extract
8 oz. vodka or brandy

Beat egg yolks and add to sugar in a double boiler or nonstick pan. Slowly add milk, vanilla and ½ of the wine. Heat and stir as mixture thickens to remove any lumps. Bring to a boil slowly and simmer for 5 minutes, stirring to prevent scorching. Remove mixture from heat and stir while cooling. Add remaining wine and all alcohol. Pour into a bottle and seal tightly. Shake it well. Mature for about 6 weeks and it is ready for drinking.

Yield: 4-5 cups

INDEX